The American Family Farm

The American Family Farm

A Photo Essay by GEORGE ANCONA   Text by JOAN ANDERSON

Harcourt Brace Jovanovich, Publishers

San Diego   New York   London

Library of Congress Cataloging-in-Publication Data
Ancona, George.
The American family farm/a photo essay by George Ancona: with text by
Joan Anderson—1st ed.
p.   cm.
Summary: A pictorial essay of the American family farm, focusing
on the daily lives of three families in Massachusetts, Georgia, and Iowa.
ISBN 0-15-203025-5

1. Farm life—United States—Juvenile literature. 2. Agriculture—
United States—Juvenile literature. [1. Farm life.
2. Agriculture.] I. Anderson, Joan. II. Title.
S519.A53   1989
630 .973—dc19   88-30068

Printed and bound by Tien Wah Press, Singapore
First edition   A   B   C   D   E

HBJ

Special thanks to Farm Aid for their work on behalf of the
family farmer and for their contribution to this book. If you
wish to support their efforts and learn more about farm
issues, please contact them at the following address:

Farm Aid, Inc.
21 Erie Street, Room 20
Cambridge, Massachusetts 02139

1-800-FARM AID

To J. Allan Anderson

A good man leaves an inheritance to his children's children.
Proverbs 13:22

—G.A. and J.A.

Introduction

Several years ago, the U.S. Department of Agriculture announced that an American farm was going out of business every six minutes. Newspapers were filled with hard luck stories predicting the demise of the family farm. So we set out to document this important institution before it all but disappeared. What began as a tribute to a dying way of life turned into a journey of discovery and hope.

We were in search of family farmers—people who run their farms themselves without hired help. But we were also searching for individuals who were able to thrive in times of adversity—people who were surviving the daily trials of working the land by being resourceful.

After learning as much as we could about the broad range of farms in America, we decided to focus on three families: the MacMillans of Massachusetts, who operate a dairy farm; the Adamses of Georgia, who run a chicken farm and belong to a cooperative; and the Rosmanns of Iowa, who own an organic hog and grain operation.

These three families have a lot in common. They were raised on farms and learned much of what they know from their ancestors. They get genuine satisfaction out of seeing hay in the loft, silage in the silo, canned food lining the cellar walls, and newly plowed fields. Their lives are dictated by weather patterns, seasons, the needs of their livestock, and the demands of their land. Most of all, they love what they do and are determined to continue.

The MacMillans
of Massachusetts

Mist hovers over the rolling Massachusetts countryside, and the silence of early morning is interrupted
occasionally by the moo of a hungry cow. Spanning
the horizon, a strip of deep pink sky heralds the
beginning of a new day.

It is five A.M. at the MacMillan dairy farm where
the two hundred and fifty cows that occupy their
two massive barns are waiting for the first milking of
the day.

Douglas MacMillan and his son Raymond have dressed in the darkness, grabbed mugs of coffee, and by dawn have arrived in the barn. They attach milker units to the cows' teats and watch as the warm white liquid flows through clear tubing into large pails. Raymond then pours the milk from these pails into a dumping station.

"We get 5,800 pounds of milk a day," Doug says proudly. Father and son share a life revolving around growing the crops to feed the cows that in turn produce the milk the MacMillans sell for public consumption.

"Every day I know just what I have to do," says Douglas MacMillan, "and it's been that way for fifty years."

Robert MacMillan, Douglas MacMillan's father

"It feels good to be carrying on a tradition my father started," Doug says, referring to his Scottish immigrant background. "He used to say that as long as I worked hard, had some cows and some land, I'd never starve, and he was right."

Douglas MacMillan will tell you that farming can't really be learned in school. "You have to be born into it, and then absorb it." He hopes his children are doing just that.

Doug and his wife, Marilyn, bought their ninety-five-acre dairy farm from the elder MacMillans eighteen years ago. As the family grew, the children began to work alongside their parents. Today, three of the five share in the farm labor.

The family includes son Rob and his wife, Luanne, son Ray, a bachelor, daughter Sharon and her husband, Charlie, son Russell, who works in town but occasionally stops by to help out, and daughter Helen, who is away at college during the school year but who works very hard when she's home in the summer.

The MacMillan farm is truly a "family farm," because all of the labor required to run it is supplied by the MacMillan family.

"We work twelve to fifteen hours a day," Doug says. "Can you imagine what it would cost me to pay hired hands for all that overtime?"

"We're pretty much self-sufficient," says Marilyn. "We produce most of what we eat. Why, I haven't done a big grocery shopping for over two weeks. And one thing I've never bought since marrying Doug is milk."

Everyone in the family will tell you that Marilyn is the cornerstone of the farm. Up with her husband each morning, she manages the finances, does the washing, prepares all the meals, and even takes time to mend hurt feelings when necessary.

A list of chores hangs in the kitchen: burn brush, repair fences, repair barn roof, spread fertilizer, mow and chop hay, repair manure spreader.

"Most of the work gets done," she says cheerfully. "But you don't become a farmer unless you like to work hard."

Many nights Marilyn sits hunched over the checkbook trying to figure out what necessities the family can afford to buy with the money coming in from the sale of milk and what purchases will have to wait until next month.

"If all the cows are producing up to capacity and feed prices remain stable, then we can pretty much order what we need. Trouble is, we can't control the price we get for milk. It really hurts knowing we sell our milk for twenty-three cents a quart, and the supermarket sells the same amount for seventy-four cents. Somebody is getting a profit, but it's not us!"

On summer and fall days Marilyn can be found with her grandsons, Keith and Dougie, picking vegetables from her garden.

"Everything we grow goes from the garden into the pot," she says as the children load up their baskets with squash and potatoes and take them to the pantry.

Nearby, Doug is looking for "prizes," as he calls them, in his potato patch. "Digging up potatoes is worth more to me than getting a good milk check. I can't help being excited every harvesttime." He stops and leans on his hoe for a minute. "Remember how we planted seeds just a few months back?" he asks the boys. "And then, just five days later, all those rows of little green corn plants came popping up? Oh, it was beautiful!"

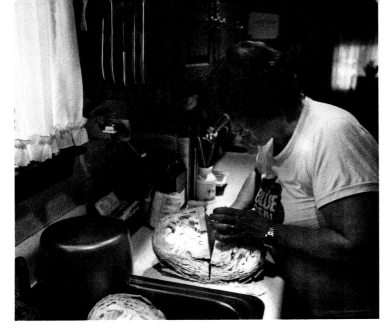

Although each family has a house, Doug and Marilyn's kitchen is the hub of all activity—a place to meet and plan. As the various family members arrive for lunch, Marilyn takes the calendar off the wall and asks the men about the farm's progress. She records which fields have been cultivated, how many bales of hay were stored away, which cows are due to calve, how much feed needs to be purchased, and so on.

During the meal, the conversation is full of genuine satisfaction stemming from daily achievements around the farm.

"Ray and I were noticing," Rob says, "that no one is getting better corn than we are this year."

"And I bet we'll have a bumper hay crop to boot," Charlie adds, much to the pleasure of Doug, who sits at the head of the table.

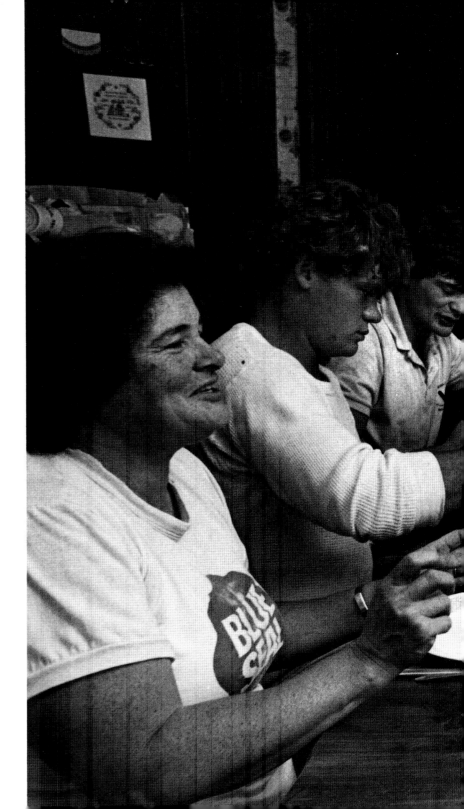

After lunch, Rob and Luanne head across the yard to the red clapboard house they share with their son, Dougie, and their two daughters, Jaime and Jen. Married to Rob six years ago on a nearby hilltop, Luanne, who is new to farming, sees great value in their daily life.

"Friends and relatives who come to visit end up becoming part of the place," she says, cutting up MacMillan apples for a pie. "And there's no stopping our daily routine, ever. I've learned that you can make all the plans in the world, but if the corn has to be chopped, you just have to stay and do it. Why, my husband even delayed taking me to the hospital to have our son until after the cows were milked!"

"I love what I do," Rob says. "When I was a kid in school, I never could understand why I had to be inside when I could be out on the tractor or working in the barn, and I suppose my son, Dougie, will feel the same way. He's starting off just like me."

Rob is an exceptional mechanic and can repair and rebuild most of the big machinery on the farm. Having attended an agricultural college, he has a broad understanding of farm management and even designed the MacMillans' new barn.

"Everyone has a specialty here," he says.

"I spent four years in the Navy seeing the world," Ray MacMillan says, "but I couldn't get farming out of my blood. I like the freedom it offers, although lately that freedom is being threatened."

Ray is referring to newly proposed legislation that would impose additional rules and regulations on the handling of farm animals. "It's scary to think of having to answer to people who don't know much about farming," he says, shoving manure out of the mangers and cleaning each stall to keep the area free of bugs and bacteria.

"Inspectors come regularly to make sure our barn is clean," he says. "Farmers are always having to conform to outside standards, it seems."

A happy-go-lucky guy, Uncle Ray, as the children call him, is always ready to pull two or three nieces or nephews up onto the tractor and head off to fertilize a field.

However, he's also quick to point out the disadvantages of dairy farming.

"A couple of weeks ago we lost one of our best cows after she calved. Two days later, we lost another. You feel real sad," he says. "Each cow has an identity of her own, and we get attached to them. Besides that, each loss means money down the drain."

Every day at the MacMillans' second barn, son-in-law Charlie is busy with the morning milking. On school days his wife, Sharon, stops by to drop off their younger son, Keith, before leaving for her teaching job in town.

"I don't know of many jobs where a father can have such close contact with his children," Charlie says. "Our two boys have been coming to the barn since they were ten days old.

"Sharon and I began to build up this herd before we even thought of buying a house or raising a family," adds Charlie, an expert herdsman who has a strong interest in cattle breeding. "You feel a real sense of accomplishment when a heifer calf turns out to be twice as productive as its mother."

Working alongside his father, Keith shovels feed and helps coax the cows out to pasture.

In the afternoon, Sharon returns with older son, Ian, and the whole family tends to the barn chores.

"Throwing hay is my aerobics class," Sharon says. "I have to admit that on bad days I sometimes wonder why we keep to this crazy schedule, but then I think of all the time we share—working and playing and riding the tractor, and I tell myself, *this is good*."

The care of animals is a skill taught to farm children at a very early age. Keith and Ian are responsible for feeding the barnyard kittens and a pen full of rabbits, too. Jaime loves bottle-feeding the calves as her cousins play nearby atop their miniature John Deere tractors.

"We teach them early how to handle the machinery," Rob MacMillan says, smiling as he watches his son at play.

In farming no day is predictable. Everything hinges on uncontrollable factors such as weather, soil conditions, human error, and equipment breakdowns.

Right now the fields are bursting with hay and corn, the main staples needed to feed the dairy cows. If the MacMillans can harvest a good crop from these fields, they will need to buy only grain, minerals, and molasses to add to their cows' diet.

"Our goal each year is to fill all three silos—the towers where we store the corn until it is needed," says Rob.

Each fall the corn is cut and chopped by a machine the MacMillans attach to their tractor. Corn particles spew into a wagon and are hauled back to the barns.

The corn wagon is parked alongside the silo, and the men rake the chopped corn, or silage, onto a conveyor belt that travels to a giant blower pipe outside the silo. The silage is then sucked up into the top of the mammoth tower.

When it's time to feed the cows, Ray opens a trapdoor at the bottom of the silo and fills a cart with the silage that pours out. In all, the MacMillans' three silos hold 1,500 tons of feed.

Many times during the harvest season, Marilyn and Luanne do the barn chores because the field-work takes the young men away for long periods of time. Their daughters join them after school.

"We all fill in to help each other," Marilyn says. "The big jobs are a team effort."

There is an old adage which seems to apply to the way the MacMillan family operates: "A farmer prospers by hard work, the grace of God, and a good wife."

"If we didn't pitch in, we'd never see our husbands," Luanne says as she dumps feed into the hog pen. She and the others rake manure out of the stalls and scatter hay they have pitched from the loft. Marilyn spreads sawdust around to absorb dampness and odors in the barn while Jaime and her grandfather haul feed from the bin.

It is not unusual to find the men still unloading silage by moonlight, long after the day is done. Tonight they are especially late because the wagon got stuck in the mud, and it took two tractors and several hours to free it.

"One thing you learn on the farm is to be patient," Luanne says. "We're always waiting for something— a calf to be born, feed to be delivered, the hot weather to break, and, of course, the men to come to dinner."

During harvest season, when the days are long and the nights even longer, the MacMillan women keep supper hot and try to be ready to nourish tired spirits.

"How are you doing? Are you still breathing?" Marilyn asks Doug, who had to do the milking alone tonight when his sons didn't return from the fields in time. On nights like this, Doug can't help but think that they work terribly hard for a very small profit.

Nevertheless, Doug MacMillan and his boys always feel a sense of accomplishment as they walk home, regardless of when their day ends.

Every other day the milk truck arrives from the dairy to collect the MacMillans' milk.

To determine the butterfat content of the milk, the driver first takes a sample out of the cooling vat where it has been stored. She then attaches a hose to the vat to draw the milk into the tank truck that will take it off to the dairy.

"We're paid according to the butterfat content," Doug says. "The higher the butterfat, the more valuable the milk, because that's what they use to make cream and butter. We have to be very careful to control what the cows eat so they produce a high quality product."

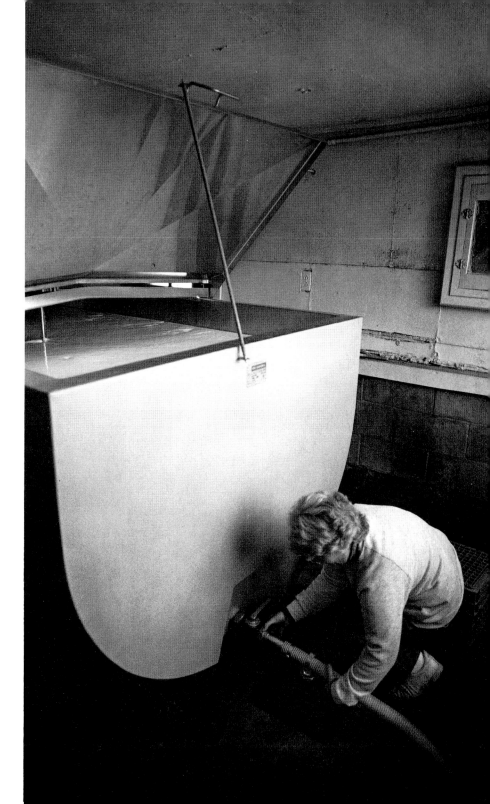

"Times are bad now for the farmer, but times were bad even when my folks had the farm," Doug says. "We won't go out of business because we're not making enough money. Things are tight, that's for sure, but we've learned to cut costs and not overextend ourselves. There's a lot we do without. My barn isn't automated, for instance, and Rob recycles old equipment for us. Even so, I don't have much time to worry about it—no matter what, the cows need milking twice a day. You've just got to keep moving forward. If you treat the land right and you treat the animals right, they'll respond."

The Adamses of Georgia

Willie Adams's house and farm in Greensboro, Georgia, are tucked away behind the towering pines that line the east Georgia highway.

"At the fork in the road, bear left," Willie says, "and go down the hill and over a bridge. You'll see our sign. The house is at the end of the road."

Willie lives with his wife, Linda, daughter, Shonda, son, Cedric, and his mother, Rosie.

"I spent my childhood following my grandfather as he steered the horse-drawn plow and worked these ninety-two acres," Willie says. "In those days, the fields around here were full of cotton, peanuts, and corn."

Despite hard times, Willie's grandfather did whatever was necessary to hold onto the land.

"Then, when I was just fifteen, he took ill and could no longer work," Willie remembers, "and things had to change if the farm was to survive."

"That's how I eventually got into chicken farming," he says. "There was no way I could manage growing crops and go to school at the same time. Besides, with synthetic fiber becoming more and more popular, cotton was on its way out. My mother and I were forced to change our way of farming altogether."

They phased out crops and began raising beef cattle, improving their pastureland to allow them to feed the new herd. Twelve years ago, Willie added two poultry houses to his farm. "In this business you always have to look ahead to what will sell. Poultry farming doesn't depend on weather, because the chickens are kept in specially built houses. As long as they are fed properly, you're pretty much guaranteed a healthy chicken at the end of eight weeks."

"We live a simple life—real quiet and peaceful," says Rosie, sitting on the porch with her grand-children on her lap. "There's always a breeze on this front porch, because the house sits on a little knoll and catches the air.

"It sure is a perfect place to raise children. Lets 'em see down-to-earth living. That way they learn how things are. Living on a farm allows you to go down to grass roots and know that something can always be created from the soil."

Every day, Cedric sets off for the fields with his red wagon.

"He collects whatever is growing out there," his grandmother says. "Willie did the same thing when he was little, and look what happened to him!"

Everyone has a place here. Linda Adams tends to the poultry houses when her husband is off in the fields. In the afternoon she says good-bye to the children and goes to work in a nearby sock factory.

"Most of the women out here work away from the farm at least part time," she says. "It adds a steady income for us, along with what we get from the chickens. If farming is in your blood and you want to stay on the land, you do what needs to be done to make that possible."

Twice daily, Willie drives five miles in his pickup truck to a tract of U.S. Forest pastureland where his seventy Beefmaster cattle graze. "I rent the land for a small fee," he says. "It's one way the government is trying to help the small farmer.

"Here in Georgia the cattle can stay out all year long," Willie says as he unloads buckets of feed. "They're good animals. I wouldn't feel like a farmer if I didn't have a herd of cows."

"A few years back something very exciting happened to me," says Willie. "I began meeting other black farmers who seemed to love agriculture as much as I did. At the time, we were all struggling, working independently of each other. Most of our wives had jobs, and none of us could afford hired hands. Gradually it occurred to me that perhaps we could help each other, that surely there would be strength in our combined ideas. And so I formed a cooperative in which the members would experience a sense of kinship, share knowledge and labor from time to time, and offer each other moral support—just like it would be if we were brothers working the same farm. The co-op is like an extended family farm."

Today ten members, all of whom share common roots, belong to the cooperative. They are Willie and Linda Adams, I. V. and Annie Henry, Leroy Cooper, Melvin Cunningham, Roger Lemar, Frank Smith, Robert Williams, and Mrs. E. M. Neal.

Descended from Africans brought as slaves to this country over one hundred years ago to till the white man's land, these fifth-generation farmers truly know the cycles of agriculture.

Willie is in constant contact with the co-op members, discussing individual needs and problems and trying to make arrangements for one farmer to help another.

"We share large machinery, trailers, and trucks for hauling livestock," he explains. "We save a lot of money by not owning identical equipment." The members are always on the lookout for used equipment that can be bought inexpensively and restored for communal use.

"Some of us are better mechanics than others," Willie says. Today he is calling Melvin Cunningham to repair his tractor, and in return for his time Melvin will use the tractor to work his land. Similarly, Willie recently borrowed a truck from one of the co-op members to pick up seeds a feed store was giving away. He managed to get enough to be able to share them all around.

The members also share animals. Willie drives twenty miles over to Oncone County to Frank Smith's farm in order to make arrangements to use his prize bull for breeding.

Frank's chicken and cattle farm is a bit smaller than the others. "I bought this land right out of high school," Frank explains. "I wasn't quite as lucky as the other members of the co-op, who inherited farmland. There was nothing for me to inherit except the wise words of my great-grandmother, who was a slave. She used to say: 'Make the best better, and then you can't go wrong.'"

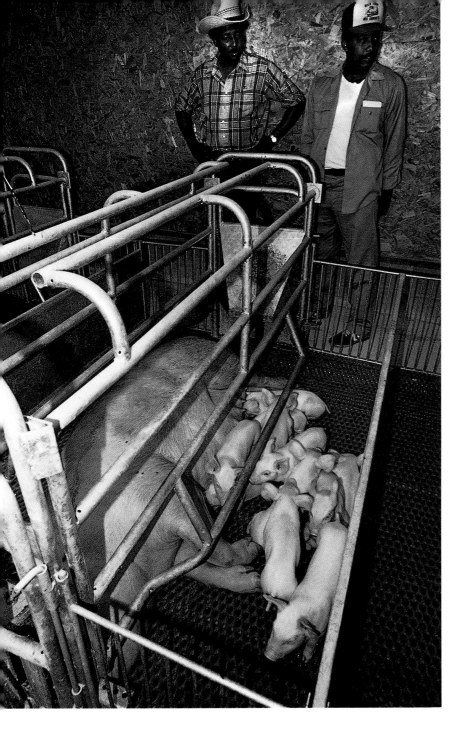

Leroy Cooper, who owns the largest farm in the co-op, also lives in Oncone County. He has six poultry houses and a huge hog operation and is always looking for ways to improve his herd.

Today Leroy is showing Willie his newly built barn with special pens for nursing sows. The pens are built to confine the eight-hundred-pound mothers so they won't crush their piglets when they try to suckle.

Nearby is Leroy's son, who seems more than comfortable handling the piglets.

"I hope he'll see that this is a good life," Leroy tells Willie.

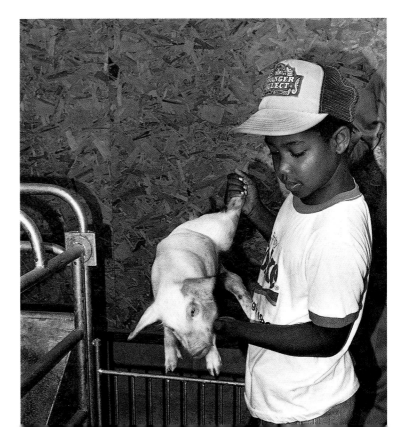

"I still dream of dairy farming," Willie says as he drives through Putnam County, the dairy county of Georgia, and pulls up to Roger Lemar's place. "It was my first goal as a child. But I soon learned it was more time-consuming than other kinds of farming because of the milking schedule."

Willie is greeted by Roger and his father, Charlie Lemar, who built their cement block milking barn back in the early fifties. Charlie Lemar taught his son the business, and Roger has expanded it threefold.

"We started with fifteen acres, and now my sixty cows graze on one hundred and thirty-five!

"Because it's been so difficult to show a profit in farming, a lot of our kids moved to the city," explains Roger. "I realized that by modernizing and expand-ing we might be able to reap larger profits and in doing so attract the kids back to the land. The co-op has helped by giving us access to the latest informa-tion on farm management and loan opportunities."

Willie talks milk prices and inquires about borrowing the Lemars' cattle trailer. The sweet smell of fresh milk permeates the air as ten cows at a time are led into stalls and hooked up to milker units for the second milking of the day. Contentment radiates from Roger's face as he works.

"I spent ten years away from this," he says, "and I'm glad to be back. It provides a peace of mind that I like. I don't enjoy punching a time clock and having people standing over me. Here it's just me and my father."

This being June in Georgia, it is time for the first cutting of hay. Willie is off to I. V. Henry's place, hoping that I. V., who owns the only baler in the co-op, will have time to harvest one of Willie's fields.

Willie finds his friend ready to hook the baler to his tractor, and he goes to help. I. V. then takes off across the broad field, where freshly cut yellow hay waits to be gathered up into massive round bales. "Round bales can sit out in the fields longer," I. V. says, "because the hay is gathered in such a way that it is better protected from the elements. Good thing, too, because none of us has enough loft space to store the square bales, which need more protection.

"This baler is an amazing machine," he adds, pleased to have found it secondhand. "It gathers the hay in a round formation and ties it together with twine in the process. Machines like this one make farming a whole lot easier than it was in the old days."

I. V. Henry has been a farmer since he was ten years old. His parents separated at that time, and he had no choice but to take up the chores of his father. "I learned early on that if you could raise it you didn't have to buy it," he says. "Since the only income most black folks had back then came from picking cotton, we learned real quick to use our extra land to raise anything and everything we wanted to eat.

"Even today, things aren't that easy," I. V. continues, running his hands through a barrel of grain. "We never know whether a bank will give us a loan or turn us down. And on top of that, there are lots of folks out there who are anxious to buy us out. With the co-op we can figure out our options better."

Because I. V. is Willie's closest co-op neighbor, the two men frequently help each other with heavy chores. In a few weeks, I. V.'s chickens will have matured, and Willie will help him herd them into boxes on turn-over day.

"Chicken farming is a one-man job until the day we ship them out," I. V. says. "Then we need all the help we can get. After the birds are gone, the entire house must be cleaned within twenty-four hours to prepare for the new shipment of baby chicks."

Weary after a long day, I. V. pauses to reflect a moment. "You know, Booker T. Washington once said: 'No race can prosper till it learns that there is as much dignity in tilling a field as in writing a poem,' and I think he was right."

"We're out to beat the statistics that say black farmers are losing their land at a rate of 9,000 acres a week," says Willie. He and his cooperative have found a way to perpetuate a lifestyle, preserve the land of their forefathers for future generations, and prosper in the process.

The Rosmanns of Iowa

A hot June breeze blows across the plains of western Iowa, where wide open spaces are divided into squares of green and yellow and pickup trucks kick up clouds of dust as they roll along narrow roads.

There is a sense of rootedness here where crops grow out of the rich black soil and sturdy farmhouses seem eternally linked to the land.

This is where Maria and Ron Rosmann work their four hundred acres of soybeans, corn, alfalfa, rye, and oats.

"Common sense is a good term for my kind of farming," says Ron Rosmann as he stands proudly beside his wife, Maria, and three sons, David, Daniel, and Mark.

Ron helped to form an organization called the Practical Farmers of Iowa, which advocates farming without using artificial fertilizers and pesticides.

"It wasn't a hard decision to make," he says. "I never liked working with pesticides—always knew they were dangerous. And since I've switched to rotating my crops and using composted manure, my harvests have been every bit as good."

The land on which his hog, cattle, and grain farm stands belonged to Ron's parents. "I was lucky to inherit well-cared-for land when my father died, and that's why I'm able to have a successful farm. I hope to pass on healthy land to my sons someday."

Everywhere you look on a bright summer day, tractors and plows are crisscrossing the Midwestern landscape. It is a productive season for the farmer. "I try to be a partner with nature," Ron says, "paying attention to her clues and working with her."

Because chemicals aren't killing the weeds in his fields, Ron must work harder. "There is more labor involved when you farm organically, but I have the satisfaction of knowing that my crops are pure and the soil is healthy."

Spending the day alone atop a tractor gives Ron plenty of time to think.

"You've got to have a lot of faith to be a farmer. Right now I'm hoping for rain. Next month I'll wish away hailstorms and tornadoes. Everything we do depends on the weather, and nature can be pretty cruel sometimes."

Maria and the boys often come out to the fields to bring Ron lunch or a cool drink. Today there is quiet concern on Maria's face as she looks at the wilting crops and dry soil that remind her of the ongoing drought.

Ron has been saying that if they don't get rain in the next two weeks they could lose fifty percent of the corn. Maria, who manages the family finances, knows as well as Ron that if they have to buy corn to feed the animals there will be a great strain on their budget.

"How's it going?" she asks her husband.

"The soil looks pretty good, Maria," he answers, to her surprise. "It's holding the moisture. We must be doing something right."

Just then, Maria reaches into a leaf and gently picks out a ladybug.

"These little bugs eat the harmful insects that chemicals used to kill for us," she tells the boys. "We didn't have them when we were using herbicides."

Today Maria Rosmann is happily adjusted as well as committed to their way of life. She manages an extensive garden and reaps the benefits of the apple and cherry trees that she planted ten years ago. "I freeze and can all our vegetables and fruits and make juice from the apples and grapes. I know I'm not making money, but I sure am saving it."

Maria's days are spent caring for the children, running the household, taping a daily radio show that reports rural news, and working in her garden.

"When I married Ron and moved out here from the city, words like *silage* and *compost* weren't in my vocabulary, but I learned pretty fast," she says, chuckling at what was at first a very lonely experience. "The day after we were married, Ron was out doing chores before I even woke up!"

Also working at the Rosmanns' farm is Ritch Hoddap, Ron's only hired hand, who today is busy feeding the 1,000 hogs a mixture of homegrown oats and corn. "Uncle Ritch," as the boys call him, not only supplies much-needed labor but is also a source of male companionship for Ron.

"Technology changed farming," Ron says, "and not always for the better. With big machinery, farmers could handle more land with less help. But farming suddenly got really lonely. Everyone was working on their own, inside their fancy air-conditioned rigs, and getting a lot done, but the sharing and neighboring was gone. I couldn't stand working without Ritch."

"Hogs are our bread and butter," Ron says, "but they take an awful lot of managing. Disease spreads quickly through the hog houses. You can lose eight to ten animals in a heat wave without even trying."

Suddenly he notices three dead piglets in a nearby pen and jumps in to pull them out. "We turn our backs for a minute," he says, frustration in his voice, "and a sow crushes her babies. I thought they wouldn't get on top of each other since it's so hot. Every pig we lose represents a hundred dollars gone. But that's farming. There's always something being born and something dying on the farm."

"C'mon, David and Daniel," Ron calls to the boys on a very hot June afternoon. "We'd better get down and water the hogs."

Since hogs don't sweat, the only way to cool them off is by spraying them with a hose. The process can be risky, however. "If a cool breeze should come through right afterward," Ron explains, "they can get a chill and develop pneumonia very easily."

Later that day the boys help their father sort out those hogs ready for market. Ritch and Ron go through the pens and mark the ones that look big enough to sell. Then they chase the marked animals, nudging them with a stick from pen to pen until they are together in one place.

"We need all the people we have when we open the gates and herd them up to the holding pen," Ron says. "David and Daniel are pretty helpful when the time comes.

"We hope our children are absorbing our life," he continues, "and that they will never grow out of wanting to bond with the land."

Sometime during the day, the men take a break from their work, especially if a neighbor drops by. This summer the conversation is filled with concern over the drought and rumors of rising grain prices. If the current grain crop is small, the price of stored grain goes up. Then farmers will rush to sell off their hogs and cattle to avoid the high cost of feeding them.

Occasionally Ron will come across one of his neighbors cultivating a connecting field late into a summer's evening.

"We are always looking at each other's land," Ron says, "checking to see how clean the fields look." A good farmer keeps his fields clean by cultivating and weeding them often.

"We don't share out of our back pockets," says Ray Errett, Ron's neighbor and a fourth-generation Iowan farmer, "but we do share ideas and time and equipment."

This year, although the surface of the Rosmann soil looks parched, Ron digs down a couple of inches and is relieved to find dampness. A graduate in biology from Iowa State University, he spends a great deal of time studying the chemistry of his soil.

"When you don't use chemicals," he says as he examines the color and body of a soybean leaf, "you become a better observer, constantly evaluating conditions and checking your product." He is continually sampling the soil from each field to make sure the nitrogen, potassium, and phosphorous levels are high enough. "Organic ground can hold more water because the soil texture has a greater water-holding capacity," he says, relieved for the moment.

"Our life is lived in cycles," says Ron as he digs his pitchfork into the manure pile that will supply nutrients for all of his land. "Each season brings different demands. We plant in the spring and harvest in the fall. Some of the crops are sold, and the rest are stored to feed the animals. They in turn provide us with food and supply the fields with manure that makes the soil fertile again and ready to receive new seeds."

The contentment in his voice seems to come from being part of a place where plants, animals, and people are all working together.

Already accepting of his parents' way of life, David Rosmann helps his mother raise evergreen trees. In Iowa, these trees are needed to shelter houses and property from prairie winds and to prevent soil erosion. The seedlings they produce are sold for an extra source of income.

"I could work day and night," says Ron while storing his hay in the loft of the barn his grandfather built. "They say he shingled the roof of this place by moonlight because he couldn't find time during the day.

"I guess I come from a long line of hard workers," he continues, as bale after bale comes tumbling off the conveyor belt. "Even after my dad took sick, he got up every day and advised me on how to manage things. When he was dying I went to visit him in the hospital and asked what I could do for him. His answer was short and simple: 'Just get back to work, that's all.'"

Like most farmers, Ron Rosmann likes being his own boss. He has never had to work for anyone other than his father or other family members. "I guess I got kind of spoiled for a job in the city," he says.

Maria and Ron are trying to hold on to a traditional way of life. Most farmers' wives have left the farm for a job in town, but Maria is committed to being a full-time wife and mother and to sharing in the farm responsibilities wherever possible.

"We'd go crazy, though, if we didn't get off the property once in a while," she says. And so, occasionally, the family piles into the pickup and heads off for an adventure. On summer evenings, they might go fishing at a nearby pond. Other times they will go into the town of Westfalia, population one hundred fifty, to buy supplies at Wehr's Feed Store and get some ice cream at the local diner. And every Sunday they can be found in church. Strongly guided by their Catholic faith, the Rosmanns are active members of the local parish, where a statue of Saint Isidor, the patron saint of farmers, looks out over the countryside.

"We believe we're caretakers of the land," Maria says, "and we must treat it with reverence."

"I'm determined to survive out here," Ron says looking out over the land where he toils so hard. "And when I hear talk of the greenhouse effect—the fact that weather patterns are changing and the world is getting hotter—I am more adamant than ever that we have chosen the right course by working with nature. We all need to realize our relationship to the earth. We are made out of the soil. Her strength lies in us and our strength ultimately comes from her."

Afterword

We made the last of our visits to these family farms in the late spring and early summer of 1988. The Adamses and the MacMillans were gearing up for the first cutting of hay, and the Rosmanns couldn't have been more pleased with their oat and rye crops. The growing season was in full swing, and all three families were in good spirits.

Then disaster struck. The entire nation was hit by a heat wave that wouldn't go away, and with it came drought. Within a matter of weeks, green fields turned yellow, corn stalks began to bend and wilt, dairy cows stopped producing milk, and many animals died from lack of water. Grain prices rose nationwide and live-stock prices plummeted. Farmers were forced to slaughter their animals because they couldn't afford to feed them. The entire Midwest was declared a disaster area. Overnight the hopes and dreams of a bountiful harvest had been erased for a multitude of farmers.

We were especially worried about the three families who had become our friends. Were they surviving the devastating drought that was putting hundreds of family farms out of business? Finally we called them at the end of the summer to see how they had been affected.

Their news was uplifting!

"We had two small rains that came just when we needed them," Maria Rosmann said, explaining that with diversification something always seems to survive. "The rye and oats came in before the drought, and

with grain prices high, we might even make money."

Although Willie Adams didn't get a second cutting of hay, the drought broke early enough in Georgia so that the pastureland was looking good, and he expected his cattle would have enough feed.

It also rained just in time in Massachusetts, and the MacMillans actually harvested a record 2,700 bales of hay. "We lost eight cows that would never have died in ordinary times," Marilyn said, "but we managed the others well—putting them out to shady pastures and cutting a hole in the barn to let any breeze inside."

In one of the worst years for American agriculture, it was almost unbelievable that we should choose, out of the thousands of farmers in the United States, three who prevailed despite the drought.

One of the reasons all three families survived is luck. As we had learned so well, weather controls the farmer's life, and, compared to so many others, our friends had been fortunate. But they also survived because they are realists—they have experienced adversity in the past and will continue to face it in the future. "It's part of the profession," Doug MacMillan will tell you. "You just learn to work through the problems."

The MacMillans, the Adamses, and the Rosmanns all seem to possess an indomitable spirit, not unlike the pioneer spirit of early Americans. Their sheer *will* to survive fuels their desire to search constantly for new and better ways to remain on the land and maintain a lifestyle that they cherish.